EARLY PEOPLES

THE INCA

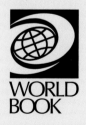

WORLD BOOK

World Book
a Scott Fetzer company
Chicago
www.worldbookonline.com

World Book, Inc.
233 N. Michigan Avenue
Chicago, IL 60601
U.S.A.

For information about other World Book publications, visit our
Web site at http://www.worldbookonline.com or call
1-800-WORLDBK (967-5325).
For information about sales to schools and libraries, call
1-800-975-3250 (United States), or 1-800-837-5365 (Canada).

Library of Congress Cataloging-in-Publication Data

The Inca.
    p. cm. -- (Early peoples)
  Includes index.
  Summary: "A discussion of the early Inca, including who the people
were, where they lived, the rise of civilization, social structure, religion,
art and architecture, science and technology, daily life, and entertainment
and sports. Features include timelines, fact boxes, glossary, list of
recommended reading and web sites, and index"--Provided by publisher.
  ISBN 978-0-7166-2135-5
  1. Incas--Juvenile literature. I. World Book, Inc.
F3429.I563 2009
985'.019--dc22

                        2008033320

Printed in China by Leo Paper Products Ltd.,
Heshan, Guangdong
2nd printing June 2010

STAFF

TABLE OF CONTENTS

Glossary There is a glossary on pages 60-61. Terms defined in the glossary are in type **that looks like this** on their first appearance on any spread (two facing pages).

Additional Resources Books for further reading and recommended Web sites are listed on page 62. Because of the nature of the Internet, some Web site addresses may have changed since publication. The publisher has no responsibility for any such changes or for the content of cited sources.

WHO WERE THE INCA?

The Inca were a native South American people who ruled a huge empire in the Americas. The heart of this wealthy empire was the region around Cusco *(KOOS koh)*, or Cuzco, a city in a valley of the Andes Mountains in what is now southern Peru. A network of roads linked Cusco, the Incan capital, with the rest of the empire.

Founded in the 1430's, the Inca empire extended over 2,500 miles (4,020 kilometers) along the western coast and mountains of South America. It included parts of present-day Argentina, Bolivia, Chile, Colombia, and Ecuador. The lands ruled by the Inca included rain forests and harsh deserts and stretched from high mountains to beaches along the Pacific shore.

The Inca were not the first people to settle in this part of the Andes Mountains. Several other groups had lived there earlier, including the Wari *(HWAH ree)*, sometimes spelled Huari, and the Tiwanaku *(tee wahn AH koo)*, also spelled Tiahuanaco.

▼ Machu Picchu *(MAH choo PEE choo)*, which was probably an Incan royal estate, stretched along a ridge between two mountain peaks more than 7,710 feet (2,350 meters) above sea level. It is one of the greatest archaeological sites in the world.

▶ A golden plate crafted by the Inca depicts the sun. The Inca's most important god was Inti *(EEN tee)*, the sun god. The plate is now in the collection of the National Museum in Lima, Peru.

HOW DO WE KNOW?

Some ancient **cultures** of the Americas, such as the Aztec and Maya, had a written language. Modern scholars have learned much about these cultures through the writing their people left behind. Not so for the Inca, who did not have writing. The only records left by the Inca are knotted strings, called **quipu** *(KEE poo)*. As far as archaeologists know, the Inca used quipu only to record numbers and dates.

Some of what we know about the Inca is based on accounts written by Spanish conquistadors and Catholic missionaries. Most of these accounts were told from the Spanish point of view and show little understanding of Inca life. In addition, much information has been lost because the Spaniards generally tried to destroy beliefs and practices that they felt went against the Christian religion. Other accounts, written long after the conquest of the Inca, depended too much on memory. In addition, nearly all of the information the Spaniards recorded about the Inca came from Incan **nobles**. As a result, we know very little about how commoners lived, or about life in areas far from Cusco.

Our best information about the Inca comes from archaeological **excavations.** Archaeologists have made many important discoveries when excavating at sites ranging from palaces to simple farms.

Starting in the early 1400's, the Inca began to conquer neighboring kingdoms. Over the next 100 or so years, the Inca built the largest empire of any American Indian people. **Archaeologists** believe that from 3.5 million to 7 million people lived under Inca rule.

The mighty Incan empire came to a sudden end in the 1530's. Spanish **conquistadors** *(kon KEES tuh dawrz)*, or soldier-explorers, arrived in Incan lands. Led by Francisco Pizarro *(frahn THEES koh pee THAHR roh* or *frahn SIHS koh pih ZAHR oh)*, the conquistadors killed the Inca's ruler and captured Cusco. However, it took about 40 years for the Spaniards to complete the conquest of the Inca.

WHAT WERE THE MAJOR ACHIEVEMENTS OF THE INCA?

The Incan empire existed for little more than a century. Yet, in that brief time, the Inca overcame many obstacles to become the most powerful group in South America. The Inca used both military skill and **alliances** to bring dozens of other groups into their empire. They combined religion and government to rule people who far outnumbered them.

Ruling such a vast territory required great practical skills as well as military strength. The Inca built a network of roads that linked every part of their empire. These roads made it possible for goods, messengers, and soldiers to move easily from one area to another.

Incan cities were carefully planned. Temples and palaces display remarkable construction skills, particularly for cutting and fitting huge stones together. The Inca even used their building skills in their farming. To grow crops on the region's steep mountainsides, the Inca carved out **terraces**, or flat

▲ Ruins at Ollantaytambo *(oh yahn tay TAHM boh)*, a palace northwest of Cusco, showcase the excellent stonework used in Incan buildings.

STUNNING SIGHT

In 1911, American explorer Hiram Bingham III stumbled upon the site of Machu Picchu, a complex of buildings high in the mountains northwest of Cusco (see photo on page 4). Bingham was stunned by what he saw:

"Surprise followed surprise in bewildering succession. I climbed a marvelous stairway of granite blocks, . . . and came to a clearing in which were two of the finest structures I had ever seen. Not only were there blocks of beautifully grained white granite, the ashlars [squared stone blocks] were of Cyclopean [very large] size, some 10 feet [3 meters] in length and higher than a man. I was spellbound."

◀ ▼ The Incan empire stretched over 2,500 miles (4,020 kilometers) along the western coast and mountains of South America and included parts of what are now six modern countries. Cusco, the Incan capital, was located near the center of the empire, in modern-day Peru.

steps of land. The terraces helped to prevent rain from washing away soil and seeds. The leveled land was also easier to irrigate.

The Inca were highly skilled at shaping gold and silver into beautiful objects. They also made fine pottery, colorful **textiles**, and elaborate headdresses and capes of feathers.

Although they did not have an alphabet, the Inca had a way of keeping records. They used knotted string called **quipu** to keep track of the people and animals in an area. The quipu were also used by people trained in interpreting them to help remember stories from Inca **myth** and history.

THE ORIGINS OF THE INCA—EARLY ANDEAN CULTURES

People in the Andes began to farm about 10,000 years ago. The first crop that Andean peoples **domesticated** was beans. They soon learned to grow gourds, **quinoa** *(KEE noh ah* or *KEEN wah)*, a root crop called oca, and squash. People in the Andes learned to grow corn by about 6,000 years ago. They also domesticated the potato, the most famous food to come from this region.

By about 3,500 years ago, the people of the Andes had domesticated the llama and the alpaca. These animals, and the guinea pig, were raised for their meat. Llamas and alpacas were also prized for their wool. Additionally, llamas and alpacas—South American members of the camel family—carried goods along the region's mountainous roads.

JAGUARS IN STONE

A well-known early Andean culture, the Chavin, existed at the site known today as Chavin de Huantar *(chah VEEN day HWAHN tahr)*, in Peru. From about 1000 to 500 B.C., Chavin de Huantar and other similar sites became the focus of Andean culture. Chavin de Huantar had a **pyramid** that was full of rooms and passageways. Images of animals, such as jaguars and birds, were carved into the stones that made up the buildings at this site.

▼ Incan farmers plant and tend their crops on **terraces** cut into the region's steep mountainsides.

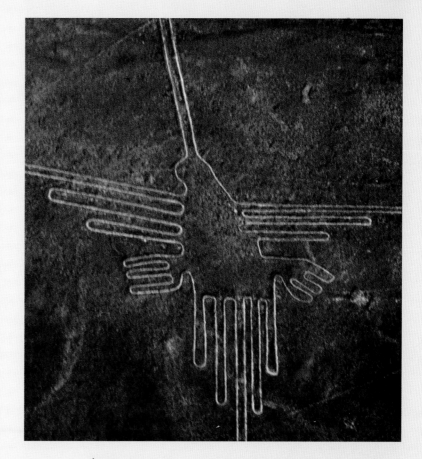

Timeline of Andean Civilization

10,000–3000 B.C. Archaic period

3300–1000 B.C. Mix of cultures, including the North-Central Coast civilization

1000–500 B.C. Chavin culture

100 B.C.–A.D. 800 Moche and Nazca cultures in coastal lowlands

A.D. 600–1100 Tiwanaku and Wari cultures in highlands

A.D. 1000–1438 Inca people begin to rise in highlands

A.D. 1150–1450 Chimu kingdom in lowlands

A.D. 1438–1532 Inca empire begins and spreads

▲ Nazca lines are huge figures etched into the desert of southern Peru. Some are more than 400 feet (120 meters) long. They depict animals, such as a hummingbird (shown in an aerial photo above), people, and geometric shapes. This hummingbird figure stretches more than 165 feet (50 meters) in length. The Nazca made the markings by removing dark surface rocks to expose light-colored sand underneath.

The oldest Andean **civilization** is known to **archaeologists** as the North-Central Coast civilization. It arose in the river valleys and nearby Pacific coast of western Peru about 3000 B.C. Archaeologists believe this civilization, which ended about 1800 B.C., was one of only six civilizations in history that developed without influence from outside societies.

Another pre-Inca Andean **culture** was the Nazca (*NAHS kuh*), which arose about 100 B.C. The Nazca are famous today for the patterns of lines, animals, and abstract shapes they marked into the ground.

In the A.D. 100's, another powerful state, the Moche (*MOH chay*), emerged. The Moche lived in the coastal desert of present-day northern Peru. They built large temples and made beautiful pottery.

Around A.D. 600, two newer states emerged in the Andean highlands—Tiwanaku and Wari. Tiwanaku was home to more than 20,000 people. Many Andean peoples thought that Tiwanaku—like nearby Lake Titicaca (*TEE tee KAH kah*)—had sacred power. The people of Tiwanaku and Wari built the first Andean empires.

When these empires declined, their place was taken by the Chimu (*chee MOO*). The center of the Chimu realm was the city of Chan Chan (*CHAHN CHAHN*). All of these early Andean cultures contributed to the culture of the people of the Inca empire.

THE INCA BEFORE THE FOUNDING OF THEIR EMPIRE

The Inca arose in the area around Cusco, northwest of Lake Titicaca, in the A.D. 1000's. They were not the only people to live in what is now southern Peru. Nearly 20 groups lived in the region at the time.

The Inca, like other groups around them, had sometimes lived under the control of the larger states in the area. Before the rise of the Inca empire, the land around Cusco was a province of the Wari empire, formed about A.D. 600. The collapse of the Wari empire in about A.D. 1000 created opportunities for various local rulers to increase their power. Among these were the Chimu, who came to dominate what is now northern Peru. Groups to the south, such as the Inca, also took advantage of the Wari's decline to expand their own kingdoms.

▼ Tall, decorated walls of dried mud mark the boundaries of one of the large compounds that made up Chan Chan, the capital of the Chimu kingdom. The Chimu reached the height of their power in the early 1400's before being conquered by the Inca. Chan Chan, which covered more than 14 square miles (36 square kilometers), was the largest city built in South America before the arrival of Europeans in the late 1400's.

▲ Mountains flank the hills and roads of the Sacred Valley of the Inca, north of the Cusco valley. A rich farming region during Incan times, the valley still supports many towns and cities.

The **culture** and social organization of the Inca helped them to thrive in the area around Cusco. Early Incan society was centered on family groups called **ayllus** *(AY loos)*. Every Inca belonged to such a group. Each ayllu owned a section of land, holding it in common for all members of the group. The leader of the ayllu determined how the people would work the land and which members would be assigned to perform the various tasks.

Villages were established throughout the region inhabited by an ayllu to take advantage of differences in climate and soil at different altitudes (heights) up the mountainsides. For example, corn grows better at lower altitudes, but potatoes thrive higher up. The ayllu placed some of its members at each growing level. The villages within an ayllu traded their farm products with one another. In this way, the people were able to obtain a variety of foods.

The Inca began to expand their rule over neighboring groups through **alliance** and warfare. By around 1400, they had shifted from a group of loosely associated ayllus to an empire.

WHAT'S IN A NAME?

The Inca called their empire Tawantinsuyu *(tah wahn teen SOO yoo)*, which means *The Four Parts Together*. The word *Inca* did not refer to everyone living in the Andean empire. The term referred only to the ruler and other members of the royal family. After the Spaniards conquered the Inca empire, they began using the word *Inca* to refer to all the native people living there.

THE FOUNDING OF THE EMPIRE

The Inca began fighting neighboring peoples in the 1300's. At first, the Inca attacks were simply raids. Inca leaders and soldiers took food or valuable goods from the other settlements and returned to the Cusco valley.

According to Inca **legend**, during the rule of Viracocha *(vee rah KOH chah)* Inca, the Inca people began to expand their territory. (Viracocha Inca took his name from the Incan creator god, Viracocha.) Initially, the Inca moved to the south. By gaining control of the flat land of the plateau near Lake Titicaca, they gained access to the region's large herds of llamas and alpacas.

Expansion continued under Viracocha Inca's son, Inca Yupanqui *(yoo PAHN kee)*. Yupanqui saved the Inca from an invasion by a nearby people. He then launched a series of military campaigns that greatly expanded Inca lands. When he took the throne, Yupanqui assumed a new name, Pachacuti *(pah chah KOO tee)*.

Several factors led the Inca to expand their reach beyond the Cusco valley. One was a desire for wealth. They moved into regions that held such precious metals as gold and silver, delicate and colorful bird feathers, and valuable shells. These riches benefited the ruler and high-ranking Inca leaders. Ordinary soldiers also gained possessions when they helped conquer rival peoples.

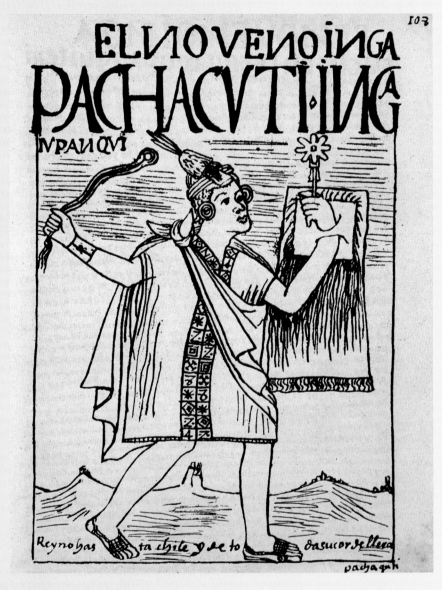

▲ A drawing of Pachacuti as he was imagined by the Andean native historian Guaman Poma *(gwah MAHN POH mah)*, who wrote an account of the Inca empire and its people in the 1580's.

The Inca gained control over other peoples in several ways. In some cases, they used military conquest. Sometimes, however, the Inca also formed **alliances** with other groups. This was particularly the case with **ethnic groups** with whom they felt closer ties. Inca rulers often strengthened these alliances by marrying women from leading families in the allied group.

Expansion did not end with Pachacuti. His son, Topa (or Tupac) Inca Yupanqui (*TOH pah EEN kah yoo PAHN kee*), continued to add to the empire, as did later rulers. By the time the Spaniards arrived in the 1530's, the Inca empire covered much of the length of the Andes Mountains and extended down to the Pacific coast.

CHANGING TIME

The name *Pachacuti*, taken by Inca Yupanqui, had a special meaning. The word described the way the Inca viewed the world. Pachacuti means "a turning over of time and space" as well as "earth shaker." A pachacuti was an event that signaled the end of one cycle of history and the beginning of a new one. By taking this name, the new ruler was declaring that his reign marked the start of a new period in history.

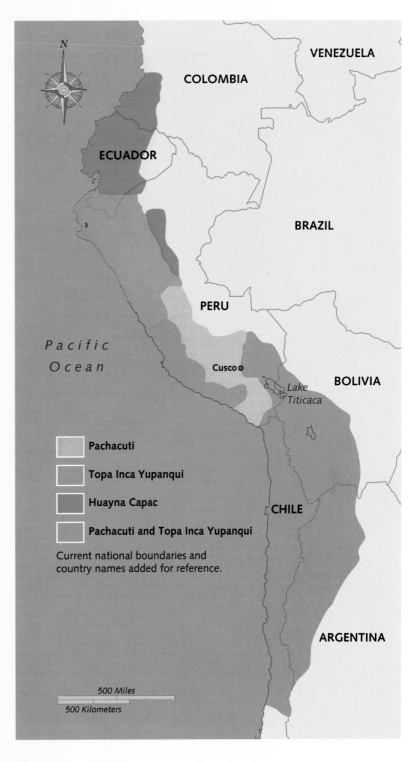

▲ Inca rulers, beginning with Pachacuti and his son Topa Inca Yupanqui, greatly expanded Inca control over vast regions.

SAPA INCAS

▶ An oil painting by a Peruvian artist of the 1700's imagines Manco Capac, one of the legendary founders of the Inca people.

The Inca ruler was called the Sapa *(SAH pah)* Inca, which means *Sole Inca* or *Unique Inca*. The Sapa Inca was always a member of the royal family. The Inca believed that the royal family could trace its ancestry back to Manco Capac *(MAHN koh KAH pahk)*. In Inca **legend,** Manco Capac was the first Inca ruler.

The Inca believed that the Sapa Inca was more than an earthly ruler. He was also the physical representation of the gods, particularly Inti, the sun god and the most important god in the Inca religion. Inti was believed to be the father of Manco Capac. Because all other Inca rulers were descended from Manco Capac, the Inca believed their rulers' ancestry could be traced directly to Inti.

RULER	DATES
Manco Capac	Legendary
Sinchi Roca	Legendary
Lloque Yupanqui	Legendary
Mayta Capac	Legendary
Capac Yupanqui	Unknown
Inca Roca	Unknown
Yahuar Huacac	Unknown
Viracocha Inca	To 1438
Inca Yupanqui (Pachacuti)	1438–1471
Topa Inca Yupanqui	1471–1493
Huayna Capac	1493–1525
Huascar	1525–1532
Atahualpa	1532–1533

Inca rulers had many wives, but the chief wife, the **coya** *(COH yah)*, was more important than the rest. As the Sapa Inca represented the sun, the coya represented the moon. The coya was also a member of a royal family. In fact, she was a sister or first cousin of the Sapa Inca.

In 1609, El Inca Garcilaso de la Vega *(gahr see LAH soh day lah VAY gah)*, the son of a Spanish soldier and a **noble** Inca mother, wrote a history of the Inca empire called *The Royal Commentaries of the Inca* (1609). In this book, Garcilaso de la Vega states that the tradition of marrying a sister began with the first Inca ruler, Manco Capac. This marriage custom was said to have started so "there should be no alteration in the purity of this royal blood that . . . they said was the blood of the Sun." Some historians, however, think that it was not until Topa Inca Yupanqui that the practice of marrying a female relative began.

Some Inca rulers had as many as 100 wives in addition to the coya. These wives came from Inca noble families or were the daughters of the leaders of other peoples.

The position of ruler was not always necessarily passed from father to son. Although the ruler had to be of royal blood, he could come from one of the many branches of Manco Capac's descendants. The ruler could name his successor, but the act of naming an individual did not guarantee that that person would rule. Some who were named successors were murdered or defeated in civil wars. Others ruled briefly but were then overthrown.

▼ The Incan royal family rides in a litter, in a reproduction from *New Chronicle and Good Government* (1615), a description of Andean life and the evils of Spanish rule by Guaman Poma, an Andean native.

NOBLES

Just below the Sapa Inca in status were the **nobles.** Experts think there may have been different systems of organizing the nobility that fell away during the course of the empire's history. At the time that the Spaniards arrived in the empire, however, the social structure of the nobility was arranged as described here.

▼ An Inca warrior in a feather headdress holds a spear in an image from a painted wooden vase made between the A.D. 1100's and 1500's. Nobles played a major role in the Inca army, leading troops into battle and carrying out the emperor's orders.

The Inca had three ranks of nobility. The **panaca** *(pah NAH kah)* formed the highest-ranking group of nobles. The panaca included all the descendants of a Sapa Inca. On becoming Sapa Inca, a new ruler became the core of a new panaca that would include his descendants. There is some evidence that the panaca existed before the formation of the empire, and that families were added and removed from the rank of panaca. There were a total of 10 panaca when the Spaniards arrived.

The panaca played a special role in the Inca social system. When someone became Sapa Inca, his lands were cared for by his panaca. After the Sapa Inca died, the members of the panaca continued to perform that duty. They were also expected to care for the Sapa Inca's **mummy.**

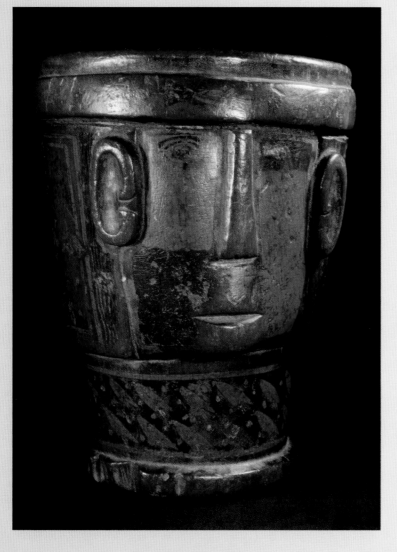

◀ A wooden kero *(KAY roh)*, or drinking vessel, decorated with the face of a nobleman. The Inca often carved keros that depicted human faces.

Members of the Sapa Inca's panaca filled the highest military and government posts. They also had some influence over the choice of a new Sapa Inca. In some cases, a panaca disputed the Sapa Inca's choice and led a revolt to advance a different candidate.

Members of the second rank of nobles were related to the royal families but less closely. Members of this group might include the offspring of a Sapa Inca's secondary wives, for example. While not of royal rank, these nobles also held high offices. In this way, they helped govern and also fought to expand the empire.

"LONG EARS"

The Spaniards called the Incan royalty and nobles *orejones (OH ray HOHN ayz)*, meaning *long ears*. This name was based on the custom among Incan nobility of piercing the earlobes and wearing golden spools as earrings. The weight of the spool stretched the earlobe. Over time, the Inca replaced each spool with a larger and heavier one. This stretched the earlobe even farther.

The panaca were divided into two groups—Hanan *(HAH nahn)* Cusco, or Upper Cusco, and Hurin *(WHOO reen)* Cusco, or Lower Cusco. The Sapa Inca could come from either Hanan or Hurin Cusco. Indeed, the first five Sapa Incas came from Hurin Cusco, and the last five from Hanan Cusco. Generally, the families of Hanan Cusco had higher status in the decades before the Spaniards arrived in the 1530's.

The third group of nobles consisted of Inca by Privilege. These people were the highest-ranking members of other **ethnic groups** that lived in the Inca empire. People could become Inca by Privilege if they joined the empire by **alliance.** This practice seems to have been designed to convince leaders to agree to place their people under Inca rule without a fight.

PRIESTS

Inca priests were vital to Inca society. The Incan government based its right to rule on a religious idea: They believed that the Sapa Inca was the representative of the sun god, Inti, and so ruled by divine right. The state religion surrounding Inti evolved many religious practices. The year was full of ceremonies honoring Inti and the other gods. Priests were needed to take part in these ceremonies and to tend shrines and holy sites.

Like **nobles**, the priests held different ranks. The highest was the High Priest of the Sun, who was probably only second to the Sapa Inca in power. This priest had the important task of confirming the person chosen as Sapa Inca. The High Priest of the Sun came from one of the royal **panaca**. Thus, he might also play a major role in choosing a new Sapa Inca. In some cases, the High Priest was also an important military leader.

CARING FOR THE ROYAL MUMMIES

Some priests attended to the needs of the mummies of dead rulers and their **coya,** or queens. For example, these priests might provide food for the mummies. The royal mummies would be taken to the main square in Cusco, where priests would lay food before them. They then burned the food on a fire, allowing the mummies to "feast" on it. The priests who cared for the royal mummies also took the mummies to other shrines for "visits" and to important festivals. Through the efforts of these caretaker priests, Sapa Incas and coya lived on in the community long after death.

▲ A sacred rock carved in the shape of a serpent's head was likely used for ceremonies honoring the gods. Liquid poured into a hollow (filled with blue stone) ran along the jagged channel from the serpent's mouth.

The rank of the other priests depended on the importance of the temple or shrine where they served. These priests took part in ceremonies and sacrifices. Priests were not just limited to religious roles, however. They helped to advise rulers and high-ranking officials about what actions these leaders should take. The Inca people generally did not make important decisions without finding out whether the **omens** favored one choice or another. Priests had the job of reading the omens. A priest could question the **mummy** of a dead Sapa Inca. He might consult with the spirits of a **huaca** *(HWAH kah)*, or sacred spot. Or he could read patterns—for example, in corn kernels, the leaves of the coca plant, or the movements of spiders—to determine what the future would bring.

▼ Pisac *(PYE sak)*, a royal estate northeast of Cusco, had a sacred area devoted to the sun god, Inti, and a house for the High Priest of the Sun.

COMMONERS

Inca commoners included merchants, craftworkers, and farmers, as well as the messengers and **quipu** makers who worked for the government. The labor of the common people supported the royals, the **nobles,** and the priests.

The Inca did not have a system of money. Nevertheless, the government found three ways to collect taxes. It collected a share of each farmer's harvest; it took a share of cloth goods produced; and it required men to perform some work for the state. This required labor tax was called **mita** *(MEE tah)*. For the purposes of the mita, all men were organized in groups. The Sapa Inca chose people to head groups of a thousand men or more. These lords chose the leaders of smaller groups under them.

Some commoners performed their mita by working in fields that belonged to the Sapa Inca or the priests. Others built roads, irrigation canals, and temples. According to tradition, as many as 20,000 mita laborers worked to build the Sacsayhuaman *(sahk sah HWAH mahn)*, a group of buildings outside Cusco that were eventually used as a **fortress** by the Inca.

The Inca used quipu to keep track of mita workers and the labor that each group had to supply during the year. This efficient counting had another benefit.

◀ A ceramic figure, made between the 1430's and 1530's, shows an Inca commoner at work. The tall vessel on the man's back, called an aríbalo *(ah REE bah loh),* held liquids. The man carries the aríbalo using straps stretched across his shoulders and chest.

▲ A **Quechua** *(KEHCH wah)* Indian woman leads an alpaca past the ruins of Sacsayhuaman. Alpaca are kept by common people in the Andes Mountains today, as they were in the time of the Inca empire.

The Inca could determine when an area could support more people. In such cases, people from other parts of the empire were settled there.

The merchant class in the Inca empire was not large. Because the Inca did not have money, all trade was based on barter—the direct exchange of one set of goods for another.

Skilled workers of gold and silver were the most highly ranked craftworkers. Potters, woodcarvers, and painters were also held in high regard. People from all levels of Inca society learned to weave cloth.

CRIME AND PUNISHMENT

Common people did not have the same rights as nobles. They also suffered much harsher penalties for breaking the law. A commoner who committed certain crimes could be executed. A noble who committed the same crimes would only suffer some kind of physical punishment or public shaming.

WOMEN

Other than the **coya** and the mother of the Sapa Inca, women in Inca society had a lower status than men. Most women did not take part in public life.

Within the household, however, Inca women were powerful. In some areas, women controlled the goods within the household. To gain this control, it was necessary for a woman to marry.

Marriage customs could differ from region to region within the empire. In certain areas, the single women and men lined up in the town square. Young men stated which woman they wanted. If two men spoke for the same woman, the governor of the area decided the matter. In other areas, a man spoke to a woman's parents to get permission to marry her. Marriage ceremonies also varied by region. In some areas, a young man gave coca leaves to his bride's mother. When the leaves were accepted, the couple was married. In other regions, the groom placed a sandal on the bride's foot to seal the marriage.

Once a woman was married, she went to her new home. Her duties there included caring for the house, preparing food, weaving cloth, and bearing and caring for children. In addition to performing household tasks, women worked alongside men in many kinds of labor, including farming. Among farm families, men plowed and women sowed the seed for

POWER AND ITS CONSEQUENCES

The wife and mother of a Sapa Inca were powerful women. However, they sometimes paid a price for their power. When a new Sapa Inca took control by force, these women "behind the throne" were occasionally seized and killed.

◀ A silver figure, made between the 1430's and 1530's, represents an aclla, or chosen woman. After four years of training in the House of the Chosen Women, an aclla could become a priestess who played an important role in the Inca religion.

the crop. Many women also traveled with the men in their family when the men served in the military. Women who had young children usually stayed at home, however.

A few women became **aclla** *(AHK yuh),* or "chosen women." Girls as young as 10 from different **ayllu** were selected to become aclla. The girls were taken to compounds in Cusco and outlying towns. Such a compound was called a House of the Chosen Women. There the aclla worked, ate, and slept.

The aclla were taught about the Incan religion as well as how to weave and cook. They also learned to brew the **chicha** *(CHEE chah)* used in Incan **rituals**. The aclla spent most of their time in the House of the Chosen Women. After four years of training, an aclla could become a priestess. As a priestess, she would play an important part in Incan ceremonies for the rest of her life. Other aclla were allowed to marry and give up their status as chosen women.

▼ A painted wooden vessel, made sometime between 1150 and 1550, shows an Inca woman with a long gown topped by a colorful top, or **tunic.**

GOVERNMENT AND LAWS

The Inca people called their realm Tawantinsuyu, which means "Four Parts Together." Each part, called a suyu *(SOO yoo)*, radiated out from the center of Cusco, the capital. The Inca believed Cusco was the center of the universe. Cusco itself had four quarters, and at its center was the Coricancha *(koh ree KAHN chah)*, or Golden Enclosure. The most important building in the Coricancha was the Temple of the Sun. Parts of the walls of this building still stand, though the Spaniards built the monastery *(MON uh STEHR ee)* of Santo Domingo *(sahn toh doh MIHN goh)* on the site.

Within their empire, the Inca ruled many different **ethnic groups.** They imposed order on their subjects partly by linking the power of the state with religious belief. As the sun god's representative on Earth, the Sapa Inca had to be obeyed without question.

In addition to the state religion, another means of control was the Sapa Inca's promise of protection. In return for their obedience, the Inca people received security from attack by peoples outside the empire.

The government often moved large numbers of people to different parts of the empire. Such moves helped government officials to make full use of the empire's resources. Uprooting people also displayed the power of the state. Some experts estimate that as many as 25 to 30 percent of the population might have been moved in this way.

Several groups of minor officials also served the government. Military commanders led the armed forces. Accountants and record keepers tracked the size of state-controlled flocks and the

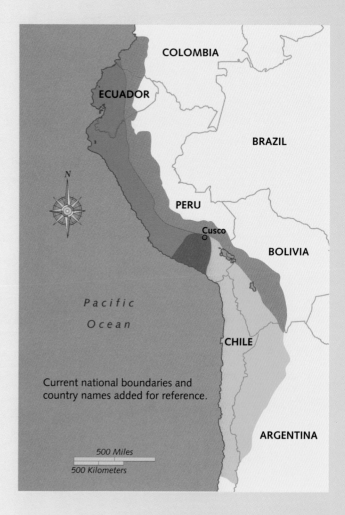

▲ The four suyus of the Inca empire.

Current national boundaries and country names added for reference.

500 Miles

500 Kilometers

CUSCO

For the Inca, Cusco was the place where the political and spiritual worlds joined. As such, it was home to the Sapa Inca and members of the royal family, to priests, and to their attendants. Few common people lived in this sacred city. Commoners came to the city only for ceremonies or festivals.

food kept in storehouses. Storytellers or amautas *(ah MOW tuhs)* taught the history and **myths** of the empire. Running on the extensive road system, messengers carried reports and other information between the Sapa Inca and others.

▲ The ruins of the Incan city of Tambo Colorado *(TAHM boh coh loh RAH doh)*, on the south coast of present-day Peru. The Inca built Tambo Colorado as a center of imperial government for the southern coast after they conquered that region. The Inca built similar cities in other newly conquered regions to establish firm government control.

CREATION BELIEFS

◀ A decorated drinking vessel, dating from around A.D. 1650, depicts an Inca creation myth. The figure in the boat is thought to represent Mama Ocllo *(MAH mah OHK loh)* crossing Lake Titicaca. Mama Ocllo is one of the eight founding ancestors in the Inca creation myth.

We know little about the Incan religion before the establishment of the empire. Most of what we know concerns the state religion that was approved by the Sapa Inca and that centered on Cusco. The Inca had many **myths** to explain their origin. Perhaps the large number of origin myths told by the Inca arose because of the empire's attempt to bring many different religious practices under one religious system over time.

In one creation myth, the Inca traced their beginning to Pacaritambo *(pah kah ree TAHM boh)*, an area south of Cusco. A mountain at Pacaritambo had three caves. The myth relates that the founders of the Inca people emerged one day from the central cave. These eight ancestors—four brothers and four sisters—moved across the land ooking for a place to settle. They carried a long golden pole that they used to test the soil in their search for **fertile** land. When they reached a hill called Huanacauri *(hwahn ah KAW ree)*, their leader, Manco Capac, heaved the golden pole into the valley below. When it sank into the rich earth, they knew they had found a place to live.

The travelers then told the people already living in the valley that they had been sent to take control of that place. In some versions of the story, the inhabitants agreed to give the land to them. In other versions, the travelers had to fight and overcome the people living in the valley. Once the Inca were in charge, Manco Capac cast corn seeds onto the land, introducing the crop that would become so important to the Inca.

In another part of the myth, two of the brothers turned to stone. One did so on the hill Huanacauri. The other did so at a place called Huanaypata *(hwahn ay PAH tah)*, which became the very center of Cusco. These two spots became sacred to the Inca.

A second Incan origin myth connected the Inca to Lake Titicaca, which many Andean peoples believed was the birthplace of the world. In this myth, Viracocha, the creator god, left the sacred lake and began walking northwest. After meeting several human beings along the way, he stopped in the Cusco valley. There he ordered that the Inca should appear.

SACRED NETWORK

The Inca had several hundred **huaca**, or sacred sites. Some were linked to springs or mountains. Others were sacred because they were connected to the royal family. Still others became sacred because they were the first spot from which a traveler coming from a certain direction could see Cusco. All the Inca's sacred sites were carefully arranged along about 40 lines that fanned out from Cusco's center. Each **ayllu** was assigned one of these lines and had to maintain all the huaca along its length. The system of lines and sacred places was so complex that one expert estimates that nearly 1,000 people in Cusco had the job of memorizing the system.

◀ The Island of the Sun is the largest of the 40 or so islands found in Lake Titicaca. The Inca built a temple to the sun and a palace complex on the island, reflecting the importance of Lake Titicaca in Incan mythology.

INCA GODS

The Inca had many gods. The major gods of the state religion centered in Cusco were Viracocha, the creator god; Inti, the sun god; and Inti-Illapa *(EEN tee ee LAH pah)*, the thunder god. All three gods were worshiped together to some extent at the Coricancha. The powers of these gods overlapped at times.

Viracocha: Although Viracocha had created the heavens, Earth, and human beings, he was not the most important Incan god. He had no priests serving him, and very few shrines were dedicated to him.

▼ A ceramic goddess figure associated with agriculture. The figure is depicted with corn (at the outer edge) and squash (covering the front). The figure dates from around the 1500's.

▶ A wooden kero, or drinking vessel, with a face carved into the front. Keros were used to serve chicha, the fermented corn beer that was featured in many Incan religious **rituals.**

Inti: The most important god was Inti, because the Sapa Inca was descended from him. As the sun god, Inti was represented by a small golden statue of a seated boy, called the **punchao** *(poon CHAH ooh)*, which meant *day.* This figure was taken from its home in Cusco's Temple of the Sun each day and returned each night. The Inca revered, or greatly honored, the punchao.

Inti-Illapa: Inti-Illapa was not only the god of thunder but also of all weather. He was responsible for rainfall. The Inca built ceremonial platforms across the landscape where they gave offerings to Inti-Illapa for rain.

Other gods were important, especially in rural areas distant from Cusco. For example, Pachamama *(pah chah MAH mah)*, the earth mother goddess, was worshiped by farmers hoping for successful crops.

The Inca believed that the world worked in pairs. Cusco and **ayllus** were both divided into what the Inca thought of as greater and lesser parts. Each half of the pair depended on and complemented the other. The sun god Inti had his complementary part in Mama-Quilla *(mah mah KEE lah)*, the moon goddess. Mama-Quilla was also important because the Inca used the phases of the moon as the basis for part of their calendar. Some experts believe that in regions outside of Cusco, and especially in areas along the coast, the moon goddess may have been more important than the sun god.

PAIRED CUPS

An important part of Inca religious ceremonies honoring the gods was the drinking of **chicha,** a corn-based beer. The chicha was served in pairs of cups, one larger than the other. The vessels used by the Sapa Inca and royals were made of gold and silver and were called aquillas *(ah KEE lahs)*. Those used by ordinary people were made of wood and were called keros. Keros are still used today across the Andes at family celebrations.

MUMMIES

▼ A female figure made of gold represents an **aclla.** Figures similar to this have been found in many Inca mummy burials. The figure is wrapped in a colorful piece of woolen cloth, which is fastened with a golden pin that resembles a flower.

The Inca are known for their **mummies**. Some of the Incan dead became mummies unintentionally. That is, no one did anything to preserve the bodies. Some people who died and were buried were preserved by the dry air and cold temperatures of the Andean climate. High-ranking people, however, were intentionally mummified after they died.

The most famous Incan mummies were royal mummies—the mummies of Sapa Incas and **coya**. We do not actually know how these mummies were produced, because no royal mummies exist today. The Inca continued to worship the royal mummies after the Spanish conquest. Spanish authorities saw mummy worship as a threat to their political power and the Christian religion. To end this threat, the Spaniards destroyed all the royal mummies as well as those of high-ranking **nobles**.

Experts on the Inca believe, however, that when royals died, priests removed the internal organs from the royal bodies. Those organs, except for the heart, were then burned. The ashes were placed in the hollow stomach of the **punchao**, the statue that represented the sun god, Inti, and the hearts were collected in a case in Cusco's Temple of the Sun. Then the bodies were set out so that the sun and dry air of the high Andes would preserve the remains.

The remains of common people were also sometimes made into mummies. Commoners as well as nobles were buried in mummy bundles. A bundle might contain one or several bodies. The mummies in a mummy bundle did not have their internal organs removed. Each body was wrapped in cotton, and it dried naturally. The mummies were also buried with clothing, food, weapons, and other

▲ Mummies and objects found at Incan burials fill a display at the Inca Museum at Cusco. The pottery vessels in the foreground held the food that the deceased person would require in his or her afterlife.

valuables. The amount and quality of the goods placed in these burials depended on the rank of the individual at his or her time of death. Inca royals were not buried in such bundles.

Some mummies represent victims who were sacrificed to the gods. In these instances, the remains were mummified naturally by the cold, dry air of the Andean climate (see page 33, The Ice Maiden).

A RACE TO SAVE THE DEAD

In the late 1980's, a few hundred Peruvians left their homes and resettled in an area outside the capital city of Lima. They had relocated to avoid a violent conflict that was being waged in other areas of Peru. The place they picked was remarkable—the site of an Inca graveyard where thousands of mummies were buried. Once they realized what was under this land, **archaeologists** sponsored by the Peru Institute of **Culture** and *National Geographic* magazine had to **excavate** very quickly to save the contents of the site before homes, schools, and roads were built there. More than 2,000 bodies held in hundreds of mummy bundles were recovered from the site. The bundles are called falsas cabezas, meaning "false heads," which refers to the headlike bulges stuffed with cotton that sit atop the bundles. Some of the bundles contain items for the afterlife, including weapons, cloth, sandals, food, and copper pins. Bodies in the graveyard date from between 1438 and 1532. The excavated mummies will eventually be displayed in museums.

Ceremonies, Festivals, and Sacrifice

Ceremonies were held at specific times of year based on the movements of the sun and moon. The largest festival was the Capac Raymi *(KAH pahk RAY mee)*. It took place at the summer **solstice** *(SOL stihs)*. In Peru, which lies south of the equator, the summer solstice occurs in December. At Capac Raymi, all the **noble** males who had reached adulthood during the previous year celebrated their entry into manhood. No commoners from outside Cusco were allowed in the city during the festival.

Another important ceremony was the Inti Raymi *(EEN tee RAY mee)*, held around the winter solstice. In Peru, the winter solstice occurs in June. On this day, because of the tilt of Earth on its axis, the sun appears at its lowest point in the sky, and the period of daylight is shortest. The Inti Raymi was held by the Inca to persuade the sun to not withdraw any farther from Earth. The ceremony took place over several days. It has been revived in recent decades. Held outside Cusco, the annual show unites traditional practices with a modern tourist-friendly spectacle.

▲ A modern reenactment *(REE ehn AKT muhnt)* of the Inti Raymi ceremony held at Sacsayhuaman, outside Cusco.

◀ The mummified body of a teenaged girl, who has been called the Ice Maiden, was discovered by **archaeologist** Johan Reinhard in 1995. The Ice Maiden was buried on a mountainside about 19,200 feet (5,852 meters) above sea level.

A CEREMONIAL SACRIFICE— THE ICE MAIDEN

Probably the most famous Incan **mummy** is known as the Ice Maiden. She was killed as a sacrifice about 500 years ago. The frozen remains of this teenaged girl were found at Mount Ampato *(am PAH toh)*, Peru, in 1995. The Ice Maiden is one of the best-preserved mummies in the world. When doctors performed a computed tomography (CT) scan on her body in 1996, they learned what had caused this girl's death. Usually such Incan sacrifice victims were drugged and then died of cold. This girl died of a head injury— she was killed with a club and then arranged in her grave. The Ice Maiden is displayed at a museum in Peru, in a glass box that maintains a cold temperature to prevent the body from thawing.

To modern minds, the Capac Hucha *(KAH pak HOO chah)* ceremony is perhaps the most disturbing. The name capac hucha means "royal obligation." This festival took place when a new ruler came to the throne or when it was time to plant or harvest crops.

For the Capac Hucha, children aged 6 to 10 (or sometimes older) from throughout the empire were chosen by local officials for their beauty. The children were sent to Cusco, along with an escort. On the appointed day, they were gathered together in Cusco's central plaza. There, each boy was symbolically married to one of the girls. Then the pairs were sent from Cusco to a sacred site. While they walked, priests chanted sacred songs.

When they arrived at the sacred site, the children were sacrificed and, in Inca belief, sent to the gods as messengers. The children were drugged before their death and most probably died of exposure to the cold. The Inca believed that the sacrificed children linked villages throughout the empire, no matter how distant, to the ruler at its center.

TEMPLES

The most magnificent of all Inca buildings was Cusco's Coricancha, a temple complex. The highlight of this complex was the Temple of the Sun. The walls of the Temple of the Sun were covered with hundreds of gold plates. The finest gold was used along the wall where the sun shone into the temple. Gold sheets of lesser quality were placed on the other walls. Each sheet was about 2 feet (60 centimeters) long and weighed about 4.5 pounds (2 kilograms). The temple also held the **punchao**, a golden altar, and a golden fountain.

▼ A Sapa Inca (center) is carried into the Temple of the Sun in Cusco, in an artist's drawing. At the left, **aclla** stand near the **mummy** of a former emperor.

THE GOLDEN GARDEN

In his history, *Chronicles of the Incas* (1540), the Spanish soldier Pedro de Cieza de León *(PAY droh day see AY zah day lay OHN)* described one of the most spectacular examples of Inca metalwork:

"There was a garden in which the earth was lumps of fine gold, and it was cunningly [cleverly] planted with stalks of corn that were of gold—stalk, leaves, and ears. . . . Aside from this, there were more than twenty sheep [probably llamas] of gold with their lambs, and the shepherds who guarded them, with their slings and staffs, all of this metal."

▲ Sunlight shines through openings in the Temple of the Three Windows at Machu Picchu.

Unfortunately, these fine achievements in metalwork disappeared as a result of the conquest. The punchao was lost. The Spaniards seized all the gold and silver they found and sent it back to Spain. They used crowbars to pull off the plates of gold that covered the walls of the Temple of the Sun. One of the greatest losses was the dazzling golden garden (see box on page 34) inside the Temple of the Sun. The Coricancha held many other beautiful things. The Temple of the Moon, dedicated to the moon goddess, Mama-Quilla, was covered in panels of silver.

A room dedicated to the Pleiades (*PLEE uh deez*)—a cluster of stars in the constellation Taurus—was, like the Temple of the Moon, decorated in silver. The Inca believed that the stars of the Pleiades were linked with the moon.

There were temples in other cities and sites across the Inca realm. All showed the finest stonework the Inca could achieve.

Machu Picchu, a mountaintop complex northwest of Cusco, has several temples, including the Temple of the Three Windows. Those windows suggest the three caves that figured in the Inca origin **myth** (see pages 26 and 27).

PALACES AND FORTRESSES

▲ Ruins of the royal estate at Pisac.

Many early **cultures** are famous for their impressive tombs full of riches. The **pyramids** of ancient Egypt, for example, continue to dazzle the world. Although they were master builders, the Inca did not have magnificent tombs. Such tombs were not needed because they did not bury their royal dead. When Sapa Incas and their wives died, they were mummified so that they could continue to take part in ceremonies.

The Inca did build large palace complexes, however, as homes for their ruling Sapa Incas. Some of these palaces later housed the royal mummies. Indeed, if a palace remained in the use of a royal **mummy,** the new Sapa Inca had to build a new palace for himself. The number of palaces in Cusco therefore multiplied. As a result, over time the most **fertile** land and the best palaces were dedicated to the dead and cared for by their **panaca.**

▲ A doorway at Sacsayhuaman, a site that was eventually used by the Inca as a fortress.

READY-MADE FORTRESSES

In the 1500's, the Inca gathered in certain complexes to resist the Spanish invaders. The Spaniards, who had difficulty ousting the Inca from these places, considered them to be fortresses. Although these complexes were almost certainly built for other reasons, they served quite effectively as defensive positions. Two of these "fortresses" that were particularly important were Sacsayhuaman, near Cusco, and Ollantaytambo *(oh yahn tay TAHM boh)*, on a mountain north of Cusco. Sacsayhuaman seems to have been built originally as a temple and religious complex. Ollantaytambo, still only partially completed when the Spaniards arrived, was a royal estate of Pachacuti, with a palace, other housing, temples, roads, and bridges. At Ollantaytambo, the steep **terrace** walls made of large stones made it impossible for the Spaniards to conquer the Inca who fought at this site.

The palaces and estates built by Incan royalty were usually huge complexes of stone buildings surrounded by a stone wall. There was often a great plaza, or open square, within a palace complex. The stonework may not have been elaborately carved or decorated, but the work was amazing. The buildings featured enormous stones closely and carefully fitted together.

The Inca also had some **fortresses,** though not as many as might be expected, given the importance of the military to the Inca. They did not need many fortresses because the Inca military usually was attacking rather than defending. No neighboring states were really powerful enough to attack the Inca. Nevertheless, the Inca did build military forts in areas where they believed that the people were likely to rise up against the Sapa Inca's authority. These walled enclosures were usually built of stone. Within the enclosure was a platform and sometimes buildings used to store weapons or food. Incan forts were not large or elaborate. Many of these forts were positioned to help the Inca control mountain passes.

ART AND CRAFTS

Inca architecture and art reflected the people's surroundings and had symbolic and religious value. The Inca cut notches into walls in such a way that the hole created a frame for a view of a mountain or valley. They carved a snake from a rock that hid an underground spring, so that the water spouted from the snake's mouth. These were all expressions of the Inca belief in the power of certain sacred places. Sculptures were often miniature versions of real locations, people, or objects. One stone in Machu Picchu was trimmed to echo the shape of the mountain peak that can be seen directly behind it. The small statuettes buried with sacrificed boys and girls were versions of the sun god and moon goddess. By creating these small-scale representations, the Inca hoped to tap into the power of the spiritual world.

◀ Geometric patterns decorate a pottery vessel that would have been used by Incas of the noble class.

LIGHT AS A FEATHER

Feathers were an important decorative element for the Inca. Iridescent (changing color when moved) feathers from hummingbirds were sometimes woven into cloth garments meant for royalty or the nobility. The Inca also made beautiful headdresses and capes of feathers, and some of the headbands worn by Sapa Incas were decorated with feathers.

▶ A solid gold llama, dating from the 1100's, was crafted by the Inca as an offering to the gods.

The Inca highly valued weaving, and their **textiles** show great craft and skill. Most textiles in the highlands were made from the wool of llamas and alpacas. In the coastal lowlands, the Inca spun cotton cloth. Cloth made by the Inca often featured bright colors and bold geometric patterns. So much cloth was required in the empire that entire towns of weavers were organized. Some of these towns held as many as 1,000 families.

Carved decorations on keros, the **ritual** drinking vessels, also show the Inca's skill. Keros were decorated with complex geometric patterns or formed into animal shapes.

Pottery was also decorated with designs. Some pottery pieces incorporated the heads or bodies of animals into handles or other parts. Certain shapes were common, including large, round containers with narrow necks and shallow food containers with duck heads. **Nobles** used pottery goods, but common people used objects made of wood.

The Inca used artistic styles as a way of exerting control. Different peoples had their own styles of pottery and sculpture, but the Inca insisted that they adopt Incan forms and patterns.

ASTRONOMY AND CALENDARS

Most complex societies based upon agriculture studied astronomy, and the Inca were no exception. Knowing the movement of the stars and planets allowed the Inca to predict the seasons. They used this knowledge to judge the best times to plant and harvest crops.

The Inca called the brightest stars chaska (*CHAHS kah*). The chaska included the planets that can be seen with the unaided eye, such as Mars and Venus. Dimmer stars were called cuyllor (*KOO ee lohr*), which means "star." The Inca recognized several groupings of stars that were also noted and named by Europeans, such as the Pleiades and Orion's Belt.

To the Inca, objects in the heavens had a connection with earthly life. Each earthly animal had a corresponding animal star or group of stars in the heavens that protected the animal. The Pleiades star group was the original source of these protecting stars, which is why the Pleiades had special meaning for the Inca. The Pleiades were also important to the Inca's calendar cycle for planting.

Some Inca temples were built in particular places to link them to the movements of the sun and moon. The Temple of the Sun in Machu Picchu has a stone called the Intiwatana (*een tee wah TAH nah*) that is mounted on a platform. The four faces of this stone are aligned with the four directions: north, south, east, and west. The stone casts particular shadows during the **solstices** and **equinoxes**. Another temple, at Vilcambamba (*veel cah BAHM bah*), has a rock opening perfectly positioned to direct a shaft of sunlight onto a particular spot at a solstice.

The Incas' knowledge of astronomy allowed them to make complex calendars, but our knowledge of these calendars is somewhat limited. Much of the information we have comes from European sources reporting on the Inca calendar after the fall of their empire. The Inca had a lunar calendar—that is, a calendar based upon phases of the moon. The names of their lunar months are given in the chart below. We also know the times of some ceremonies and activities that the Inca based upon this calendar.

▲ The four faces of the Intiwatana at Machu Picchu are aligned so that the stone casts particular shadows on the solstices and equinoxes, days of great significance to the Inca.

LUNAR MONTHS

Month	Approximate start date	Features and activities
Capac Raymi	December 23	Summer solstice; Capac Raymi ceremony
Pacha Pocuy Quilla *(PAH chah poh KOO ee khoh EEL yuh)*	February 21	Ripening of crops
Inca Raymi	March 23	Autumn equinox
Atun Cusqui *(AH toon koos KHOH ee)*	April 22	Harvest of sacred corn field
Haucay Cusqui *(hah OO kay koos KHOH ee)*	May 23	
Chacra Conacuy Quilla *(CHAH krah cohn ah KOO ee khoh EEL yuh)*	June 23	Winter solstice; Inti Raymi ceremony
Chacra Yapuy *(CHAH krah ya POO ee)*	July 23	Sacrifices to sources of water
Coya Raymi Quilla	August 23	Planting sacred corn field
Uma Raymi Quilla	September 22	Spring equinox; Coya Raymi ceremony
Aya Marcay Quilla *(AU uh MAHR kay khoh EEL yuh)*	October 22	Ceremonies to bring rain
Capac Inti Raymi	November 22	Preparing for Capac Raymi

ENGINEERING

▲ The "stone of 12 angles" in a wall at Cusco demonstrates Incan skill in masonry.

The Inca were superb masons, or stonecutters. Several things made their excellent stonework even more impressive. The Inca had to move stone great distances and up and down steep mountainsides using only muscle power, as they did not have any transport with wheels. Their walls, however, were often built with huge stones—taller than people. In addition, the Inca did not have the benefit of iron tools; they had to cut stone with stone. Finally, the Inca built lasting structures only by fitting stones. They did not use **mortar** in their constructions. Despite these difficulties, stones cut by the Inca are often, to this day, so precisely fitted that a knife cannot be inserted between them. Many walls built by the Inca have survived several earthquakes, when walls built by later peoples have collapsed around them.

The Inca had two kinds of stonework. Ashlar (*ash LAHR*) refers to stone that was cut into rectangles of the same size and then stacked. These stones were used on walls that stood alone. Impressive work in ashlar can still be seen today in a curved wall that remains from the Coricancha in Cusco.

HEAVY LOADS

The huge ashlars that the Inca used in their walls often weighed a few tons each. How did the Inca raise these stones to form a wall? Experts believe the Inca piled up earth on one side of a wall, forming a ramp at the height of the course of stones then making up the wall. The next large stone to go into the wall was moved over the earth and put into place. Then more earth was added, bringing the ramp up to the level of the next course of stone. Another course of stones was added. When the wall was finally completed, all the earth behind it was removed.

◀ Water flows through the stone channels at Tambomachay, as it has for centuries. Had the Inca used mortar to join the stones, instead of just fitting them carefully together, the water would have worn away the mortar over time and perhaps allowed the stones to shift.

The other kind of stonework used by the Inca is called polygonal *(puh LIHG uh nuhl)* and refers to stones of several shapes. Some of these shapes are quite complex, and the builders had to carefully cut pieces to perfectly fit each one next to its neighbor. One of the most impressive examples is called the "stone of 12 angles," in Cusco. Polygonal stones were used by the Inca to erect buildings.

Inca engineering skill can also be seen in their waterways. They dug canals to carry water from distant sources to fields. The sacred rivers that flowed through Cusco were lined with stone.

At Tambomachay *(tahm boh MAH chay)*, an archaeological site near Cusco, there is a spectacular series of channels that carry water down a hillside. These channels are cleverly hidden beneath stones, making small waterfalls at the bottom highly dramatic.

The Inca also used their skills to build roads of stone (see pages 52 and 53).

KEEPING RECORDS AND SENDING MESSAGES

One of the most remarkable Incan technologies was the **quipu**—the system of knotted strings that was used to record information. Each quipu had a strong main string to which many secondary strings were attached. These secondary strings were knotted in certain ways, with some twisting in one direction and others in another. Adding to the complexity, secondary strings are of different colors, and some have additional strings attached to them.

▼ Scholars have yet to unravel the secret of the quipu—the knotted strings that the Inca used for record keeping.

READING THE STRING

Scholars have about 700 examples of Incan quipus, but no one knows how to read them. A recent find of 32 quipus in a grave site provides a new opportunity. Researchers are trying to connect the quipu knots with the kinds and quantities of goods found at the site. They are also using computer programs to analyze known quipus to find patterns that can give clues to their meaning.

▶ An Incan chaski, a royal messenger, is carrying a quipu and blows a shell to signal the need for a replacement runner, in an illustration from Guaman Poma's *New Chronicle and Good Government* (1615).

The quipus were tools for accounting, ways of keeping track of the number of animals in a flock or the number of people in a village. Some scholars believe the quipus may also have been used as a form of written language—to record, for instance, histories, but that is less certain. At the very least, we do know that expert individuals who made and read quipus used their patterns to remember key people, places, and events.

Quipus were carried by the chaski *(CHAHS kee),* the royal messengers who carried news and information along the roads. Young men were specially trained for this role. Each chaski ran as fast as he could for as long as he could. Fresh runners waited at stations along Inca roads. A runner who was too exhausted to travel farther and needed a replacement blew on a shell as he neared a station. A fresh runner emerged and began running alongside him. The first messenger relayed the message, the second runner raced on, and the first runner stopped to rest. The Inca system of message runners was efficient and fast. A relay of messengers could cover an impressive 150 miles (240 kilometers) in a day.

The chaski did not just carry messages. They were also used to transport light and valuable goods, especially those meant for the Sapa Inca. Sometimes chaski brought fresh fish from the coast to Cusco.

FAMILY LIFE AND CHILDREN

The Inca usually had large families. Because so many children died in infancy, women tended to have many children so that enough children survived to help the family.

A baby born to the Inca was not coddled. As soon as it was born, it was tightly wrapped and placed in a cradle that could be strapped to the mother's back. A baby was taken out of the cradle only to be nursed and changed. Mothers did not hold their babies for long periods of time. Such treatment, the Inca thought, spoiled a baby.

Babies were nursed until they were 2 years old. Then they were given solid foods. Only then were they named during a special ceremony.

SETIMO CALLE
TOCII AROCVAMRA

BABY'S FIRST HAIRCUT
Along with receiving a name, children got their first haircut at the age of 2. It was viewed as a special event, with uncles and aunts taking part. The hair was kept and carefully guarded by the family. The Inca believed that the hair held the spirit of a person. If someone with supernatural power gained control of the hair, he or she could cast a spell to hurt the individual.

◀ A boy hunts small game with a sling, from Guaman Poma's history of the Inca people, written in the early 1600's.

The children of Inca commoners did not usually go to school. As they grew up, the boys and girls were taught by their parents. Boys were taught the trade or skill their father practiced. Girls learned how to cook, run the household, and weave from their mother.

Whether **noble** or common, the only girls that were schooled were those selected to be **aclla**. Noble boys were sent to Cusco, where they were taught by government teachers. The boys were taught Inca history and religion. They also learned how to make and read **quipu**.

At about the age of 13 or 14, children went through a ceremony that marked their becoming adults. Girls went through this ceremony alone, but boys did it in groups. Both boys and girls, however, had to fast for a few days before the ceremony. At this ceremony, they were given their adult name.

Young men married any time from their late teens to their early 20's. Young women tended to marry a bit younger. The marriage of a man and a woman bound not just the couple, but also their two families. These families were expected to support and help each other when needed.

▼ Women in the Andes still carry infants on their back, as Inca mothers did centuries ago.

HOUSING AND CLOTHING

The palaces and homes of royals and **nobles** were large and had many rooms. The buildings were made of finely cut stone and had steeply sloped roofs. The roofs were thatched—that is, covered with dried grass bound together in bundles. Thatch is still used in the Andes today.

The homes of nobles had windows and doorways. There is some evidence that these doorways held wooden doors, but no doors have survived. Many Inca doorways and windows had openings that were shaped in the form of a trapezoid (*TRAP uh zoyd*)—wider at the bottom than at the top.

The homes of common people had no windows and just one door. A leather or cloth hanging covered that entrance, providing some privacy for the people inside. Homes for the common people were fairly small. They were made of stone in the mountains and sun-baked brick in coastal areas. Like the houses of nobles, houses for commoners had steeply sloped roofs.

▶ This structure at Ollantaytambo, dating to the Incan empire, has been rebuilt and is now used as a house. It is typical of Incan building, with a steep, thatched roof and trapezoidal (larger at one end than the other) window openings.

Styles of clothing were the same for Inca people, regardless of social rank. Men wore loose **tunics** that hung down to the knee. Women wore dresses of similar length. Although styles were similar, clothing for people of different status varied in the quality of the fabric and materials used. Nobles and royalty wore clothing made of a blend of fine wool and cotton. These garments might have decorations of gold, silver, and shell. The common people wore clothes made of fairly coarse wool. The coarsest wool of all was used for blankets and bedrolls.

FINE, RARE THINGS

The Sapa Inca's clothing was specially made by the **aclla** and was of the best quality. Some of the Sapa Inca's clothes were made of surprising materials. Atahualpa *(AH tah WHAHL pah)*, the last Sapa Inca, appeared at one meeting with the Spaniards in a magnificent shirt. Asked what material it was made of, Atahualpa explained that it had been spun from the fur of bats.

▶ The rich gold plates of this tunic suggest that its owner was a noble of high rank. The Inca had laws that determined what materials people could use for clothing, plates, and drinking vessels. Only the Sapa Inca could use the finest materials.

FOOD

◀ A round Incan pottery dish holds ears of corn like those grown by the Inca. Corn was an important food throughout the Americas.

Women and girls were responsible for the food in Incan society. Preparing food took a great deal of time and effort. An important task related to cooking was gathering wood, or the dried dung of llamas or alpacas, to burn for fuel.

The Inca ate two meals a day, one early in the morning and the other at the end of the day. Inca commoners mostly ate corn, potatoes and other vegetables, and **quinoa,** a grain native to the Andes. Food was flavored with chili peppers. Sometimes, the Inca toasted corn in a fire, dried it, and then pounded the dried corn into meal that was formed into cakes.

When commoners ate meat, it was typically from an older animal that could no longer work. Because this meat was tough, it was usually stewed. **Nobles** were more likely to eat roasted meat because they ate younger, plumper animals. Coastal people sometimes ate fish, which they often cooked in a stew.

ROYAL MEALS

The Sapa Inca ate the best food from plates that were made of gold and silver. When a spot of food fell on his clothing, he rose from his meal and changed his clothes before continuing to dine. The bones from animals, cobs of corn, and other leftovers from the Sapa Inca's meal were all carefully preserved until they could be burned in a special ceremony. Burning them was thought to prevent an evil person from using the garbage as a way to cast a spell on the Sapa Inca.

The Inca took advantage of the cold, dry temperatures of the highland climate to preserve food. Left out at night, foods in the highland froze. The next day, the Inca would press and squeeze out the water left in the item and then leave it to dry in the sun. Potatoes and other goods freeze-dried like this could be stored and eaten later.

Common people did not eat all the food they produced. A share of their produce was collected by the government and held in storehouses scattered throughout the empire. These supplies fed government officials, priests, soldiers, and the **mita** laborers.

◀ Incan pottery vessels in the shapes of vegetables reveal some of the foods that the Inca ate, including corn, gourds, peppers, and squash.

TRANSPORTATION

One of the marvels of the Inca empire was its extensive network of roads. These roads covered around 24,800 miles (39,900 kilometers) and linked every corner of the empire. The Inca were not the first people in the Andes region to build roads. But the Inca's road network far surpassed what any people had built before.

The main road for the Inca was a highway that ran north and south. It

▼ To climb steep mountainsides, the Inca created roads that zigzagged back and forth.

THE INCA ROADS

When the Spaniards entered the Incan empire, they were amazed by the road system. In his book, *Chronicles of the Incas* (1540), the Spanish soldier Pedro de Cieza de León *(PAY droh day see AY zuh day lay OHN)* praised the Inca for this extraordinary engineering achievement:

"In human memory, I believe that there is no account of a road as great as this, running through deep valleys, high mountains, banks of snow, torrents of water, living rock, and wild rivers. . . . In all places it was clean and swept free of refuse [litter], with lodgings, storehouses, Sun temples, and posts along the route. Oh! Can anything similar be claimed for Alexander [the Great] or any of the powerful kings who ruled the world...?"

▲ Modern Peruvians pick their way down a mountain using carefully built stone steps. The Inca built such steps to allow travelers to climb up and down hills more easily.

stretched from a place near modern Quito *(KEE toh)*, Ecuador, to present-day Mendoza *(men DOH zuh)*, Argentina. Another road ran north and south along the coast. In some places, this road ran inland into nearby hills to skirt deserts. About 25 east–west roads crossed these main roads. The east–west roads connected highland sites to coastal areas in the west. Roads also led down the Andes in the east to plateaus and foothills. Some roads ended in the thick rain forests of the Amazon River Basin. There, the Inca traded with native peoples for colorful feathers.

Some stretches of the Inca roadway were made of stone, though rarely was the entire length of a road made of stone. Usually, at least some stretches of a road were made of tamped earth (earth packed down by pounding or pressure). The best roads were those from Peru north to Ecuador and from the central valleys to the coast. Stone steps were built into hillsides to allow travelers to climb hills more easily.

The Inca roads had to cross many rivers, some of which spanned deep ravines. Where possible, the Inca built bridges of raised earth. When the drop was too steep, they made bridges of braided plants. One spectacular example, west of Cusco, crossed nearly 150 feet (46 meters) above the Apurimac *(ah poo REE mahk)* River.

The Inca built a system of inns, called tambos *(TAHM bohz)*, along the roads. People traveling the road network could stop at the tambos for the night.

CIVIL WAR

In the early 1490's, Huayna Capac became Sapa Inca. He ruled for more than 30 years. During much of that time, the Inca were at war in what is present-day Ecuador. In the 1520's, however, the Sapa Inca sickened and died.

The son that Huayna Capac had named to succeed him also died. The son's untimely death left two rivals for the throne, Huascar *(HWAHS kahr)* and Atahualpa, who were half-brothers.

◀ Stone and iron objects that Inca warriors attached to long handles to make clubs. The iron heads on the right must have been made after the Spaniards arrived. Before then, the Inca did not have iron tools or weapons.

▲ Atahualpa,
as imagined by a
Peruvian painter of the 1700's, more than 200 years
after the death of the last Sapa Inca.

THE DEADLIEST WEAPON

When Europeans first reached the Americas, they carried diseases that were new to the region. Native peoples had no natural defenses against these illnesses. As a result, huge numbers of native people died. In the 1520's, smallpox, unknowingly brought by Spanish explorers to the coast of South America, spread to Inca lands. Hundreds of thousands of the Inca and people living under Inca rule died. Huayna Capac was almost certainly one of the victims.

Huascar was named Sapa Inca while Atahualpa was away from Cusco with the northern armies. Atahualpa sent messages to Huascar pledging his loyalty. However, Huascar quickly began to upset people in the capital. He killed the lords who had been escorting the dead body of the late Sapa Inca. All were highly placed **nobles** from Upper Cusco. Huascar killed messengers that had been sent by Atahualpa. He also outraged many nobles by threatening to burn the royal mummies and seize their estates.

Atahualpa, meanwhile, took steps that some Inca viewed as an attempt to stake a claim to the throne. Angry, Huascar decided to wage war on his half-brother. The war lasted several years. During the fighting, many of Huascar's generals abandoned his cause and joined Atahualpa's. Atahualpa had another advantage. His soldiers were more experienced fighters.

In the end, Atahualpa won. His followers then carried out a deadly revenge. They killed all of Huascar's wives and children, forcing the dethroned Sapa Inca to watch. They also burned the **mummy** of Topa Inca Yupanqui, the son of Pachacuti, and killed almost all members of this Sapa Inca's **panaca.** Huascar had belonged to this panaca.

Atahualpa advanced toward Cusco, ready to become Sapa Inca. He stopped at the town of Cajamarca *(kah hah MAHR kah)*, where he heard word of the arrival of some strange white-skinned men with beards. The men were burning villages wherever they went. Atahualpa sent one of his generals at the head of a large force to meet and defeat these intruders.

THE SPANISH CONQUEST

Pizarro (center) demands a ransom from Atahualpa (seated), in an engraved illustration from *Historia Americae* (History of America), published in 1602 by printmaker Theodore de Bry. The ransom that was eventually delivered included more than 13,000 pounds (5,900 kilograms) of gold and over 26,000 pounds (11,800 kilograms) of silver.

The white-skinned, bearded men Atahualpa heard about were **conquistadors**, led by a Spanish soldier named Francisco Pizarro. Pizarro had heard of the wealth of the Inca empire while living in Panama City. He began exploring and eventually found the empire in around 1527 or 1528. Impressed by the riches of the Inca, Pizarro returned to Spain, where King Charles I appointed him governor of Peru.

Pizarro returned to South America and set sail from Panama City with 180 men. They landed in what is now Ecuador. In 1532, they founded the city of San Miguel—now Piura *(PYOO ruh)*—in northern Peru.

In late 1532, the Spaniards met Atahualpa in Cajamarca. On November 16, 1532, Atahualpa was carried to the huge plaza in the town. With him were dozens of **nobles** and around 7,000 Inca soldiers armed with stone clubs and slings. Pizarro, meanwhile, had hidden his soldiers and a cannon in the buildings around the plaza. At his signal, the Spaniards attacked. Protected by metal armor and armed with cannon, guns, and swords, the conquistadors massacred the Inca. Thousands of Inca died, but not a single Spaniard.

During the fight, Pizarro captured Atahualpa. The Sapa Inca offered to pay a huge ransom for his freedom. He promised to fill a room to half its height with objects of gold and to fill it twice with goods of silver. Pizarro agreed. For several months, the Inca gathered the ransom goods while Atahualpa ruled his people from captivity. Pizarro, meanwhile, sent for reinforcements.

By the following summer, the ransom and the reinforcements had arrived. Pizarro finally took the advice of some followers and had Atahualpa executed. Over the next several months, the Spaniards fought several battles and won most of them. On November 15, 1533, the conquistadors entered Cusco.

The Spaniards named Manco Inca—another son of Huayna Capac—as the new ruler. It was Pizarro, however, who really controlled things.

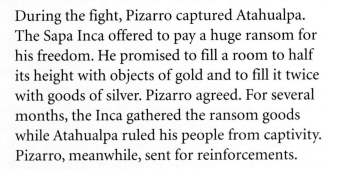

REVOLT

Two centuries after the fall of the Inca empire, a native Peruvian tried to revive it. He was related to the last Inca ruler and took a form of that name, calling himself Tupac Amaru II. He launched a revolt in 1780 that tried to recapture Andean lands for American Indians. After months of bloody fighting, he was captured and killed. Some time later, the revolt died out.

Meanwhile, the Spaniards had to fight in several areas to put down resistance to their rule. Manco Inca eventually fled Cusco and organized a resistance.

In a huge battle in 1536, the Spaniards won a major victory. Still, Manco Inca and his followers escaped to Vilcabamba *(veel kah BAHM bah)*, where the Inca continued to resist for more than 30 years. The Spaniards finally defeated this force in 1572 and captured the last ruler, Thupa Amaru *(TOO pah ah MAH roo)*. He was executed.

◀ In Cusco, the Spanish built a church dedicated to Saint Dominic on the foundations of the Coricancha of the Inca. The Incan foundations of the building can be seen below the archways of the church.

THE INCA LEGACY

Today, nearly 500 years after the fall of the Inca empire, the achievements of the Inca still hold the imagination and pride of the people of Peru. Peru's currency was once called the inti *(EEN tee)* after the Inca sun god. The name for Peruvian currency today still reflects Inca tradition. The currency is called the *nuevo sol*, Spanish for "new sun."

Nearly half of Peru's people are of American Indian descent. More than a third of the remaining people are of mixed American Indian and European heritage. **Quechua**, the language of the Inca, is also an official language of Peru. Nearly one-third of the people of neighboring Bolivia speak Quechua, which is an official language of that country as well.

▼ Three young Peruvian girls in traditional clothing pose in front of a Cusco building. Andean peoples still use many structures built in Inca times, and many aspects of their lives, from family relationships to farming practices, continue to reflect Inca traditions.

▲ Inca traditions remain alive in the textiles traded in a modern open-air market in Peru. The Inca were known for textiles that featured colorful dyes and complex patterns.

Inca traditions can still be seen in the Andes today. The Inca **ayllu** continues in the form of ties joining people into large extended families. In many highland communities, villages own the land collectively, not individually. People work together on projects for the public good—for example, to maintain irrigation canals or care for public spaces.

In cities, the Inca left their mark. Many of the most important buildings in Cusco use Inca walls as their foundations.

The influence of Inca **textiles** can be seen today in the beautiful and complex designs produced by Andean weavers.

The sacred traditions of the Inca are viewed with respect. Even today, some native peoples of the Andes still give thanks to the Inca earth mother goddess when they enjoy good harvests.

THE FIGHT OVER INCA TREASURES

American **archaeologist** Hiram Bingham rediscovered Machu Picchu in 1911. Bingham unearthed mounds of pottery, silver goods, and human remains and shipped them to Yale University in New Haven, Connecticut, where he taught. The government of Peru began demanding the return of those treasures soon after their arrival in the United States. Peru claimed that its original agreement with Bingham only allowed Yale to borrow the treasures. In 2007, the university agreed that Peru is the rightful owner of the goods and pledged to return them once a new museum is built in Cusco to house them.

GLOSSARY

aclla A chosen woman, meaning a girl who was specially trained to live in and serve the Inca religious houses.

alliance A union formed by agreement, joining the interests of people or states.

archaeologist A scientist who studies the remains of past human **cultures.**

ayllu A kinship group that was the basis of Inca society and that owned land in common for all the groups members.

chicha A corn-based beer used in Inca **rituals.**

civilization The way of life in a society that features complex economic, governmental, and social systems.

conquistador A Spanish soldier-explorer. The conquistadors conquered parts of the Americas for Spain.

coya The chief wife of the Sapa Inca. Often, this wife was the Sapa Inca's sister. The Inca, however, called many female relatives *sister*, so the coya may just have been a close female relative to the Sapa Inca.

culture A society's arts, beliefs, customs, institutions, inventions, language, technology, and values.

domesticate To gain the ability to plant and grow specific crops, rather than simply gathering wild plants; or, to tame animals so they can be kept or raised.

equinox Either of the two moments each year when the sun appears directly above Earth's equator. During an equinox, all places on Earth receive approximately 12 hours of sunlight.

ethnic group A group of people with characteristics in common that distinguish them from most other people of the same society. Members may have ties of ancestry, **culture,** language, nationality, or religion, or a combination of these things.

excavate or **excavation** To uncover or unearth by digging, or a place at which such digging has taken place, especially used of archaeological sites.

fertile Able to easily produce crops (when used about land or soil).

fortress A place built with walls and defenses, used for protection from attack.

huaca A term for any site sacred to the Inca.

legend A folk story, often set in the past, which may be based in truth, but which may also contain fictional or fantastic elements. Legends are similar to **myths,** but myths often are about such sacred topics as gods or the creation of the world.

mita Work that common people in the Inca empire owed to the government.

mortar A mixture of sand and water with lime (calciom oxide), cement, or often both, for holding bricks or stones together.

mummy A dead body that has been preserved and that still has some of its soft tissue—that is, a body that has decayed only to a limited degree. The preservation of the body may have been intentional, using artificial means, such as salts and resins. Or, the preservation may have been natural—for example, a body left in a dry, cold climate was sometimes naturally dried and preserved. In some **cultures,** both animals and people were mummified.

myth See **legend.**

noble or **nobleman** or **-woman** A person or persons of high standing in his or her **culture.**

omen A sign of future good or bad luck based upon assigning meanings to such things as dreams or events.

panaca One of the groups of royal Inca. When someone became Sapa Inca, his panaca was charged with caring for his personal estates and, later, his **mummy.**

punchao A golden statue that, for the Inca, represented the sun.

pyramid A large building or other structure with a square base and four smooth, triangular-shaped sides that come to a point at the top, or, in Mesoamerica and South America, that were flat at the top.

Quechua A language of South American Indians and also a group of peoples that speak this language. The Quechua language was spoken by the Inca and is still spoken today.

quinoa A grain plant native to the Andes Mountains that was a staple of the Inca diet. The seeds are cooked and eaten whole or ground into flour. The leaves can also be cooked and eaten.

quipu A record-keeping device made of knotted strings used by the Inca and other Andean **cultures** of South America. Quipu means knot in **Quechua,** the language of the Inca.

ritual A solemn or important act or ceremony, often religious in nature.

solstice One of the two moments each year when the sun appears in the sky at either its northernmost or southernmost position. The solstices take place in June and December. The summer solstice is in June in the Northern Hemisphere and December in the Southern Hemisphere.

terrace A small wall built by farmers to hold soil on a steep mountain slope.

textile Woven fabric.

tunic A loose, short piece of clothing that is slipped on over the head and is often belted at the waist.

ADDITIONAL RESOURCES

Books

The Ancient Inca
by Patricia Calvert (Franklin Watts, 2005)

Aztec, Inca & Maya
by Elizabeth Baquedano (DK Publishing, 2005)

Francisco Pizarro: Conqueror of the Incas
by Barbara A. Somervill (Compass Point
Books, 2005)

Handbook of Inca Mythology
by Paul R. Steele and Catherine J. Allen
(ABC–Clio, 2007)

The Inca
by Charles and Linda George (Blackbirch
Press, 2005)

The Inca
by Stefanie Takacs (Children's Press, 2003)

Inca Mummies: Sacrifices and Rituals
by Michael Martin (Capstone Press, 2005)

*Machu Picchu: The Story of the Amazing Inkas
and Their City in the Clouds*
by Elizabeth Mann (Mikaya Press, 2000)

*National Geographic Investigates Ancient
Inca: Archaeology Unlocks the Secrets of
the Inca's Past*
by Beth Gruber and Johan Reinhard (National
Geographic, 2007)

Web Sites

http://incas.homestead.com/

http://incas.mrdonn.org/index.html

http://khipukamayuq.fas.harvard.edu/index.html

http://www.machupicchu.perucultural.org.pe/ingles

http://www.metmuseum.org/toah/ht/02/sa/ht02sa.htm

http://www.mnsu.edu/emuseum/prehistory/latinamerica/south/cultures/inca.html

INDEX

Acknowledgments

The Art Archive: 5 (Stephanie Colasanti), 6 (Mireille Vautier), 12 (Archaeological Museum Lima/Gianni Dagli Orti), 16 (University Museum Cuzco/Mireille Vautier), 19 (Gianni Dagli Orti), 23 (University Museum Cuzco/Mireille Vautier), 25 (Gianni Dagli Orti), 29 (Arteaga Collection Peru/Mireille Vautier), 38 (Archaeological Museum Lima/Mireille Vautier), 39 (Archaeological Museum Lima/Mireille Vautier), 42 (Gianni Dagli Orti), 44 (Archaeological Museum Lima/Mireille Vautier), 46 (John Meek), 50 (Archaeological Museum Lima/Mireille Vautier), 54 (Museo Nacional Tiahuanacu La Paz Bolivia/Gianni Dagli Orti), 56 (Biblioteca Nazionale Marciana Venice/Gianni Dagli Orti), 57 (Stephanie Colasanti); Bridgeman Art Library: 14 (Brooklyn Museum of Art, New York), 28, 51, 55 (Brooklyn Museum of Art, New York); Corbis: 10 (Pablo Corral Vega), 11 (Robert van der Hilst), 21 (Danny Lehman), 31 (John Van Hasselt), 32 (Keren Su), 35 (John Van Hasselt), 36 (Galen Rowell), 41 (Dave G. Houser), 43 (Wolfgang Kaehler), 47 (Gavin Hellier/Robert Harding World Imagery), 52 (Francesco Venturi), 53 (Jeremy Horner), 58 (Gavin Hellier/Robert Harding World Imagery/Corbis), 59 (Gail Mooney/Kelly-Mooney Photography); Getty Images: 33 (Stephen Alvarez/National Geographic); Shutterstock: 4 (Amy Nichole Harris), 27 (Joel Blit); Werner Forman Archive: 9 (N.J. Saunders), 15 (N.J. Saunders), 17 (Schindler Collection, New York), 18 (N.J. Saunders), 20 (Museum fur Volkerkunde, Berlin), 22 (David Bernstein Fine Art, New York), 26 (British Museum, London), 30 (Museum fur Volkerkunde, Berlin), 37 (N.J. Saunders), 40 (N.J. Saunders), 45 (N.J. Saunders), 48 (N.J. Saunders), 49 (Museum of Art, Dallas); World Book: 34 (Richard Hook).

Cover image: Shutterstock (Mike Von Bergen)
Back cover image: Shutterstock (Joop Snijder, Jr.)